SHROOM TRIP REPORTS

WHAT IT'S LIKE TO TRIP ON PSILOCYBIN MAGIC MUSHROOMS

ALEX GIBBONS

Copyright © 2020 by Alex Gibbons

All rights reserved.

No part of this book may be reproduced in any form or by any electronic or mechanical means, including information storage and retrieval systems, without written permission from the author, except for the use of brief quotations in a book review.

UPDATES

For a chance to go into the draw to win a FREE book every month like our 'Stoner Themed Coloring Book' (below), and other updates on our latest books, subscribe below!

https://psychedeliccuriosity.activehosted.com/f/1

For daily posts on all things Psychedelic, follow us on Instagram @Psychedelic.curiosity

Mushrooms can heal, feed and possibly enlighten you - maybe even help save the world.

— Dr. Paul Stamets

CONTENTS

A Few Things To Note Before We Start	vii
Some Background On Psychedelic Mushrooms	ix
1. A Late Night Mushroom Trip With My Brother	1
2. Mushroom Trip Out In Nature	10
3. 4-Gram Trip Leads to Weird Hallucinations and a Series of Epiphanies	19
4. A Heroes Journey	26
FAQs	35
Also by Alex Gibbons	41

A FEW THINGS TO NOTE BEFORE WE START

First and foremost, we want to make it clear that we are not trying to romanticize the use of magic mushrooms or other psychedelics for that matter. Psychedelic compounds, even those from natural sources such as mushrooms, can be harmful to you and to the people in your life, especially when they are taken carelessly.

Should you choose to take psychedelic mushrooms, whether you want to heighten your creativity, to have a spiritual experience, or just to have fun, make sure that you don't compromise your safety, or the safety and wellbeing of the people you love. Ultimately, it's only you who can decide whether or not to experiment with psychedelics, so don't let anyone pressure you into doing it if you are uncomfortable.

Magic mushrooms are controlled substances in most nations, so it's crucial to note that there may be legal consequences if you are found in possession of these mushrooms. If, after weighing the risk, you make the decision to acquire some, please make sure that you keep them under lock and key, especially if you have children around.

Ensure that you handle mushrooms carefully to reduce the risk of overdosing. Mushrooms tend to vary in potency (depending on the species or the specific part of the mushroom), so the same dose of mushrooms may have different amounts of psychoactive compounds. Ensure that you do your research on the specific variety of mushroom that you want to take before you ingest it, in order to prevent unexpected reactions.

If you are on a prescription or if you have any underlying medical conditions, make sure that you do some research so you understand whether or not it's okay for you to take magic mushrooms under your specific conditions. You should do this to reduce the risk of negative drug interactions or the exacerbation of preexisting conditions.

As you read these stories, remember that they are for information and entertainment purposes. They are real first-person stories by people who have experienced magic mushrooms, however, the names of our contributors have been altered in order to protect their privacy.

Finally, you should note that mushroom trips can be extremely subjective and people's experiences tend to differ. Your experience may be totally different from the ones you're about to read here.

SOME BACKGROUND ON PSYCHEDELIC MUSHROOMS

Psychedelic mushrooms are special types of wild fungi that have mind-altering properties. These mushrooms contain two main psychoactive compounds: psilocybin and psilocin. Psychedelic mushrooms are also referred to as psilocybin mushrooms, magic mushrooms, or just shrooms.

The mind-altering properties of these mushrooms have been known to mankind for thousands of years. There is strong prehistoric evidence that indicates that mushrooms may have been used for both recreational and religious purposes across different continents. The Aztecs and other indigenous people in Central and South American attribute divine properties to magic mushrooms, and to date, they still use them in religious rituals.

It wasn't until the 1950s that psychedelic mushrooms were introduced to westerners. A man named R. Gordon Wasson participated in a traditional ceremony in Mexico, where mushrooms were used. He brought some of them back with him to America, and soon, the word began to spread. Magazines featured articles about mushrooms and researchers began isolating and extracting the psychoactive compounds.

Since the late fifties, the use of psychedelic mushrooms has been steadily increasing in popularity. Today, there are close to 200 species of mushrooms that are known to have psychedelic properties.

Still, mushrooms are less popular compared to other psychedelics because they are wild and seasonal. That makes them relatively difficult to acquire, but since there has been an increased interest in the substances in recent years, some sellers have learnt out how to cultivate them all year round. Some users prefer to go out in the wild and gather their own mushrooms, but before you consider doing that yourself, make sure you can properly identify psychedelic mushrooms. There are documented cases where people have eaten poisonous mushrooms thinking they were psilocybin mushrooms.

Figuring out the right dosage of mushrooms to take can be a bit of a challenge. As we've mentioned, there are at least 200 species out there, and different species have different levels of potency. In some cases, mushrooms of the same species can also differ in potency. In most cases, the psychoactive component is anywhere between 0.5 and 2 percent of the dry weight of the mushroom. Mushrooms are usually sold in dried form and doses are measured in grams.

Doses of between 1 gram and 2.5 grams are considered normal or typical; most novice and even experienced users stay within this range. Doses of 2.5 to 5 grams are considered to be strong. Those seeking deep spiritual experiences often take doses within this range. Doses greater than 5 grams are called "heroic doses", and are only taken by highly experienced users, or people who want to test the limits of this psychedelic.

Although there are lots of psychedelic mushroom species out there, *Psilocybe cubensis* is the most popular kind. It's fairly easy to cultivate and it has good potency, so many cultivators and sellers prefer it over other species of magic mushrooms. In the streets, it's sometimes referred to as "cubes".

When taking magic mushrooms, preparation is important. Some people prepare for mushroom trips by fasting. This isn't necessary, but to maximize the psychedelic effects, it's advisable to ingest the mushrooms on an empty stomach. You can eat the dried shrooms straight up, but most people prefer to rehydrate them, either by adding them to smoothies, turning them into tea-like brews, or adding lime or lemon juice. Mushroom trips typically last six to seven hours from the time of ingestion.

Psilocybin and psilocin – the two psychoactive components in magic mushrooms – can be extracted, and they are sometimes sold as stand-alone psychedelics, but for the purposes of this book, we will only focus on unprocessed, natural mushrooms.

1

A LATE NIGHT MUSHROOM TRIP WITH MY BROTHER

I have been on many psychedelic trips before, but this was my first time on magic mushrooms. My brother and I had acquired a few grams of dried mushrooms when we got back home from college, and we planned on tripping late at night when everyone else was asleep.

It was a cold night, with lots of cloud cover, so there was barely any moonlight. Looking out the window, it seemed eerily dark. At a quarter past eleven pm, all our other family members were asleep, so we started preparing our mushrooms.

The dried mushrooms were already crushed into powder when we bought them, so all we had to do was soak them in some lemon juice. I had read somewhere that soaking mushrooms in any citrus juice could reduce the come-up time, as well as the whole duration of the trip; since we only had those few night hours, we thought a short trip would suffice.

I found some lemon at the back of the fridge. I cut them then squeezed and strained the juice into 2 shot glasses. I then got my mushroom bag. There were several sachets, each containing 1.5 grams of powdered mushroom. The guy who sold them to me had said that they were a blend of highly potent species of magic mushrooms. I emptied a single sachet into each shot glass, and then we let them soak for twenty minutes or so. I could have gone higher on the dosage, but being my first time, I was a bit cautious. My brother had taken magic mushrooms before – he had taken two grams of cubes and he had a fairly intense trip – but this was his first time using the lemon preparation method, so he too didn't want to up his dosage.

After the mushroom and lemon juice mixture had soaked for a while, we topped up the shot glasses with some soda water. This was meant to dilute the mixture; I had learned that mushrooms had a horrible taste and diluting them in liquid could help it feel less unpleasant to ingest.

I glanced at the clock on the wall. It was now roughly a quarter to midnight. I took the mushroom concoction in one gulp and my brother did the same. It still tasted horrible and I had to force myself to swallow it. We immediately lay down on our beds, as we waited for the mushrooms to kick in.

In less than twenty minutes, I started to feel it. I asked my brother about it and he too seemed to feel it kicking in around the same time. My brother and I had shared a room since we were kids. Over the years, we had learned that our bedroom was fairly close to our parents' room; we never could pull any shenanigans without them noticing. So, as our respective trips began, we decided to move to the attic as we didn't want to risk attracting any attention.

There were three beds in the attic; we took two that were close together. We lay there, in silence, watching the ceiling. I started to notice that the grains in the wood, both of the ceiling and the walls, were warping and changing shape. The changes were slow and minor, but they were unmistakable.

As I paid attention to the grains, I started to feel a certain heaviness in my body. It was like a heavy load was weighing down on me; it wasn't on top of me; it was inside me. It was now pressing downwards, forcing me to sink into the bed. I felt like my body was creating a deep depression in the mattress.

My brother and I stayed silent for most of the come-up. Yet, in that silence, I felt more connected to him than ever. The silence felt deeply meaningful; like we had mutually agreed, on a subconscious or telepathic level, to refrain from distracting each other, so that we each could take in this profound experience.

After about thirty minutes of deep thought, we finally broke the silence, and we started to talk about what we were feeling and perceiving. Just like me, my brother had also experienced minor visual distortions, but not much else so far. We decided to play some music to see if it could stir things up.

I went through my music app and found a playlist of my favorite melancholic songs. I turned on music and turned up the volume. We started listening to the songs. I had heard those same songs dozens of times before, but this time around they seemed to hold a deeper meaning. As I focused on the lyrics and the notes, I realized that thanks to mushrooms, I was experiencing a certain strange clarity in my understanding of the songs.

The songs seemed sadder than normal, yet they made me feel more alive than any music I had ever heard. I couldn't help but relate this effect to my life; if a sad song made me feel this alive, maybe sadness is an integral part of life itself. Without the cold and dark aspects of life, it wouldn't be so meaningful. The songs about pain, loss, and death reminded me that happiness is only possible if there is the possibility for sadness; otherwise, how would you even know that you were happy? How could you tell you were alive? A life without difficulty is no life at all.

I was so taken by the music. Shortly after the playlist came to an end and I really felt lost. All that time listening to music, it had become a part of my reality. For the duration of that playlist, I was in a magical universe where the true meaning of life was revealed to me. When the music stopped, it was like a carpet had been swiped away right under my feet; the magic had abruptly stopped working. Without the music, there was this emptiness, which is just difficult to describe. For a while, I felt stunned; I really didn't know what to do next. My deep thoughts had come to a standstill. I would have remained in that state for much longer, had my brother not suggested that we should sneak out of the house.

I followed my brother out of the house, almost reluctantly, still, a little hung up on the music. But as soon as I stepped outside, I realized that I still had so much left to experience on this trip; the music was just the tip of the iceberg. Experiencing nature, even in this dark and seemingly gloomy night, was the truly profound and life-affirming part of the trip.

We tiptoed out of the house, walked through the woods, and went to the beach, which was less than a mile from our house. Although I couldn't see very clearly, everything felt more real than ever. I remember touching the bark of a tree as we made our way to the beach; it felt more alive than any other tree I had come across in my life. It felt soft yet rigid. It was cold yet warm. It was wet, yet dry, at the same time. Its contradictory nature intrigued me, so I decided to examine it a little closer. I looked at its bark; I could see all the minute details on it; all the wrinkles, crevices, and pores. As dark as it was, I was able to take in all the details of the tree, and I was deeply fascinated by its appearance.

When we cleared the woods and approached the beach, I realized that my body was getting even heavier than before. This time, the weight was so intense that it was throwing me off balance. It felt as if my center of gravity had somehow shifted and it was misaligned with my feet. All I wanted to do was stop in position and let myself sink into the ground. Yet, I was drawn in by the water, which looked beautiful even on a cloudy night, so I forced myself to keep moving.

The sandy terrain of the beach didn't make things any easier. I dragged my feet onwards, following my brother, who seemed to have better control of his body, and on we went towards the water.

The strange thing about all of this was that I did not feel at all intoxicated. I felt stone-cold sober; in fact, my mind was clearer than it had ever been. I wasn't staggering; it just felt like carrying my own body weight was much more difficult than it had always been.

When we got to the shore, we stood there for some time, just staring at the water, looking at a landscape we had known all our lives, through a new lens. It was breathtaking to say the least. I remember mumbling, "Wow!" over and over again, as my gaze drifted across the night ocean view. It was surreal like I saw, not just the ocean, but the whole world, for the very first time. I felt like I was standing at the edge of the universe, looking at all of existence, and marveling at its awe.

There was a slight ocean breeze and as it rushed past me, I felt like it was filling me with energy like I was receiving the breath of life itself. I almost forgot that my brother was standing next to me until he started walking along the shore. I started following him.

As I walked along, I turned my gaze back towards our house. I noticed that the inland view was very different from the ocean view. While the ocean was serene, the inland view looked chaotic. All things were moving around, independent of everything else. I stopped for a moment and it occurred to me that I was somehow the center of the universe. The houses, trees, and other features were all revolving around me, each object at its own pace and orbit. I kept standing still because I wanted to make sense of this development.

Standing there, I started to realize that I was getting dissociated from my own body. Sure, I was totally aware of the existence of my body, but that didn't seem to matter to me. In fact, it did not matter where I was at that moment, or even who I was as a person. The only thing that seemed to matter was the nature of reality, the fundamental truth of the universe. Whether accidentally or by design, I realized that I had, in fact, unlocked a boundless understanding of the universe. Everything made perfect sense: For those few moments, I had access to all the secrets of the universe, and all my questions were answered.

My thoughts were interrupted by my brother, who was now a few paces ahead, beckoning me to follow him. I picked up my pace and we headed back through the woods. This time around, walking through the woods felt quite scary. I kept thinking there was something lurking in the shadows.

By now, the clouds had parted, and moon rays came in through the canopy, but was only making the shadows a lot scarier. I felt slightly nervous, but I kept calm; my brother always had my back, so no matter what happened, I knew that it would all be okay. That thought gave in a deep sense of relief, and soon, I forgot about the shadows and started enjoying my trip again.

We emerged out of the woods onto our driveway. I noticed that the driveway looked much narrower and longer than I remembered. The sky was brighter now, so we just stood there and gazed at it. My brother told me to close my eyes, so I did.

Suddenly, my field of vision was taken over by vividly strange patterns that seemed to dance around. I tried to focus and the patterns started to settle down, and to make more geometrical sense. It now looked like a vast field of hexagons of different colors. They merged together to form a colorful array of shapes that looked like honeycombs. The shapes kept splitting up and replicating; I couldn't tell if my field of vision was getting bigger, or if the shapes were getting smaller; whatever the case, they seemed to all fit in together, forming a vast mesh.

I was so overwhelmed by these visuals; I stood there for at least ten minutes, trying to figure out if the patterns had a certain deeper meaning. I only opened my eyes when I heard a dog barking off in the distance.

My brother and I had been in a rush to get back home, but standing there on the driveway, we realized that there wasn't much we could do indoors. So we decided to go back towards the beach and hang out on the sunbathing wooden chairs.

I took out my phone, and this time, I played some music off the Spotify app. The position of the phone on the open sandy beach and the rustling breeze seemed to interfere with the quality of the audio, but even then, the music was great. It was fused into reality, just like before, but this time, my mind seemed to drift away, and the music seemed to come from a deep part of my subconscious.

I had this euphoric feeling crop up inside and I got lost in the moment. I totally lost sense of the context I was in and time seemed to move at a slower rate. I was suspended in a blissful state and washed away by the sheer beauty of the experience. I was overwhelmed by a sense of gratitude and, at that moment, I thought I wouldn't trade my life for anyone else's. I stayed in that state of mind for what seemed like hours.

At some point, we decided to go back into the house for real this time and to ride out the remainder of the trip in our bedroom. We rushed back, snuck into the house, and got in bed.

As I lay in bed, I felt like I was becoming my normal self again. My body wasn't as heavy as it was before, but I could still feel the effects of the mushrooms. I started to get lost in thought again, but this time, it was more introspective.

It occurred to me that I had more control over reality than I had thought before. "Reality is what I make of it." I thought. Since I had the power to alter my own perceptions, it therefore follows that I had the power to create reality. So far in my life, my reality was limited to only what I could perceive, but now I had in me, the power to expand it. From that moment on, I decided that my world would be so much bigger, virtually unlimited.

As I turned around in bed, I checked the time. It was a little past four am. The effects of the mushroom were starting to reduce. Even then, I felt like I couldn't sleep. I decided to take a shower; it always relaxes my body and helps me fall asleep.

When I got into the bathroom, I noticed that the stones that made up the floor seemed to expand in size, shrink, and then expand again, seemingly in a rhythmic pattern. However, after I had finished showering, I checked the floor again, but this time, there were no movements. It seemed that my visuals had finally died down.

Coming out of my trip, I resolved to trust my own judgment a lot more and to learn to make independent decisions. My one take away from the trip was that reality was subjective, so there were no rigid rules on good decisions versus bad decisions. I've always been afraid of making choices in case I made the wrong ones, but now I'm confident that even if my choices aren't perfect, the outcomes won't dictate my reality; only I can do that.

2

MUSHROOM TRIP OUT IN NATURE

I had been trying to trip on mushrooms for a while. A few weeks before my trip, I had purchased what I thought were magic mushrooms from some guy at a concert, but as it turned out, they were duds. I ingested them and nothing happened. I had been duped. I wasn't going to make the same mistake again. This time, I called up an old friend who was well connected – so to speak – and I asked him to help me get some legit psychedelic mushrooms.

My friend asked me to visit him over the weekend and he promised he would have the mushrooms when I got there. He had moved away a couple of years ago, though we always kept in touch. I had to drive up to his place on Friday evening and we decided we would both take the mushrooms the next day.

When Saturday morning came around, my friend let me in on his plan. He said that the best way to experience magic mushrooms is to take the trip out in nature. There was a National Park around half an hour away from his home and he said that we would have an epic trip if we hang out there.

Around mid-morning, we ate the mushrooms and washed them down with some juice. They were dry and they didn't go down easy, but the juice really helped. I'm not sure about the dose, but my friend assured me that it was somewhere between two and three grams. He had a sizable stash in a bag, so he wasn't too concerned with exact measurements.

We got into the car immediately after ingesting the mushrooms and my friend drove as fast as he could towards the park. I was afraid that the mushrooms would kick in while we were still on the road. Fortunately, there was hardly any traffic, so we managed to make good time.

It was a very beautiful park. There was a massive forest with several meandering streams that lead to a scenic waterfall. I had such high expectations that I was certain this would be the most wondrous day of my life. I was prepared in every way. We had both packed bags full of snacks and drinks, and the weather seemed perfect for a hike and a picnic. We left the car and walked into the park. A ranger told us to pay attention to the signs and avoid restricted areas, but we barely listened to him as we excitedly walked past.

We walked deeper into the park, and when we were out of view of the ranger and the other visitors, we decided to jump over a low wooden fence that separated the border between the public areas and the restricted area. We really wanted to go deep into nature, where we wouldn't be bothered by the noisy children who were running around all over the place.

We followed what looked like an old trail down some crevasses, and after a while, we came across huge rocks with water rushing over them. The area didn't look dangerous at all, but I suppose it was restricted because the rangers were concerned about children playing on slippery rocks.

As we approached the rocks, I realized that the mushrooms were kicking in. Everything around looked a bit distorted, and I started to worry that I would get disoriented and lose my step. We made it to the rocks just fine and sat down on dry patches that rose above the flowing waters.

As we were sitting on the rocks, I noticed that the water seemed to sparkle as it hit some stones near my foot. Upon close scrutiny, it occurred to me that this appearance was an effect of the mushrooms. The water would shimmer for a moment, but then appear normal the next second. I thought this was fascinating, so I leaned over and started to wave my hand in the water.

When the water washed over my hand, I had a bewildering sensation. It wasn't just a mere liquid; the water felt like a massive living organism with an amorphous shape. When I dipped my hand in the water, it felt like I was petting a mysterious creature that left residue all over my skin. It felt weird and thrilling at the same time. For the next quarter-hour or so, I just kept playing with the water as it glistened and crawled past me.

After sitting on the rock for a while, I was starting to feel a bit numb, so I got up and started walking around. My friend was on his feet too and he was throwing pebbles into the stream. As I strolled and skipped over the rocks, I got to one rock that seemed to have deeper and calmer waters around it. But as I was starting to admire this newfound scenery, I felt a bug zoom right past my ear.

I looked up and now there were at least two bugs flying around my head, as though they were attracted to the smell of my hair or something. They kept flying back and forth, and I thought they were really annoying. I swatted my arms at them and missed a couple of times. For a moment, I started to think it was a bit funny. I even remarked to my friend that maybe I should strip and dive into the water to get away from them. My friend laughed and pointed out that swimming in the stream wouldn't be a good idea.

In the midst of that exchange, I turned around, and I realized that the bugs had multiplied exponentially. They were all over me and they were making the air pretty dense. I couldn't make out what they were; they sounded like mosquitoes but looked as big as bees.

In hindsight, I realize that most of the bugs I saw weren't even there. Sure, there were a couple of bugs in the beginning, but the swarm of super-mosquitoes was a mushroom induced hallucination. I didn't know that at the moment, everything felt so real.

"They're all over me!", I yelled as I nervously threw my arms and legs all over the place. "What are they?", I asked.

"What are you talking about?", my friend asked. I thought his tone was really obnoxious, mostly because it didn't occur to me that we perceived reality differently at the moment.

The bugs were undeterred. It was like every winged pest known to man had decided to descend upon me and ruin my day. It started to feel as though they were landing on me. They weren't just stopping on the surface of my skin; they would burrow deep and make me feel uncomfortable from within.

By now, my friend had realized that I was having a bad hallucination, and he thought that it was really hilarious. He had been on a few bad trips himself and he didn't think they were a big deal. He thought that I would get over it in a minute, but after a while, he realized that it was getting serious. He knew he had to do something before I went down the bad-trip rabbit hole.

My friend decided to help me out, but he knew that telling me my hallucinations weren't real would probably be futile. So he decided to play into the hallucinations. He said: "Come on, I'll help you get away from these pesky bugs."

He led me away from the rocks, towards a tree under which we had left our backpacks earlier. As we moved along, we seemed to leave the bugs behind us. The whining noises in my ears seemed to get a bit distant, and now it sounded like I was haunted by the ghosts of pissed off bugs. I knew that part was over, so I started paying attention to the things that were ahead of me.

For a moment, I noticed a tree that was covered by a strange type of moss. This moss seemed to jitter and shake, like it had the ability to move about. It was like a forest creature that was trying to camouflage itself by attaching to a tree trunk.

My attention was grabbed again, this time by pine needles hanging off a group of trees along the path. The pine needles had touched my arms and now it felt like they were tentacles that were burrowing through my muscles, all the way into my bones.

We picked up our bags and we tried to trace our way back to the non-restricted area of the park, but we found ourselves going down the wrong trail. It must have been a combination of the fact that we were tripping and that we had never been to the park before. With very few identifiable things along the way, it's fairly easy to lose your way in a strange place when you are on mushrooms.

We kept following a small footpath, although we had no idea where it was taking us. We found ourselves on a different section of a stream and we decided to wade across. There were little rock islands spread across the shallow stream, but we definitely would have to step in the water to get across. My friend let me lead the way, but just as I got to the edge of the stream, I froze in place.

Looking into the water, I noticed that there were dark creatures swimming all over the place. It might have been a hallucination or nothing at all for all I know, but at that moment, I was fully convinced that the water was full of eels and piranhas, just swimming around in anticipation as they waited for me to make the mistake of stepping in the water. They were darting around, going about their business, but I knew they were just trying to fool me.

I gathered enough courage to bolt across the stream. I leaped from rock to rock, until I got somewhere in the middle. I figured I couldn't make the next step, so I stood there for a while. Looking down again, I convinced myself that the eels and piranhas were starting to crawl up the rock, so I panicked and ran back.

Seeing this, my friend asked me to step aside so he could cross first. He casually walked across, wading through the water, not at all concerned about getting his feet chewed on by flesh-eating fish. I decided to follow him as fast as I could, trying to curb my fear. I stepped into the water when he was halfway across, and I rushed to catch up with him. The water felt like molten lava flowing over my feet. It seemed more viscous than normal and I really struggled to move my legs.

As I kept crossing the stream, I realized that there was a lot of sticky sand and silt at the bottom, which was why the water felt so dense. It was as though the stream had come alive again, and this time, it was trying to drag me down into its depths. I kept going deeper with each step, and when I made it to the other end, I really had to struggle to free my legs from the grasp of the stream.

I sat on a rock at the shore and tried to clean my feet as I watched a part of the stream that was cascading over some stones, forming eddy currents. That's when I started to have deep depressing thoughts about my life.

In recent months, I had tried a few different drugs, and in my moment of depression, I started to worry that my drug use had caused irreversible brain damage. I thought that I was no longer as smart as I used to be when I was a child and that I would keep getting stupider as the days went by. I remember thinking that the anti-drug crusaders were right, that drugs killed brain cells, and caused permanent brain damage. "By now, I must have lost like 50 IQ points!", I thought. "What if I can't do anything smart for the rest of my life? What if my parents found out that I like to experiment with drugs?"

As those depressing thoughts set in, I felt a horrible taste in my mouth, so I spat across an adjacent rock. The spit looked like highly concentrated acid that was burning its way through the rock.

I turned my attention to my hand, which had a blister. I had burned my thumb a few days before, and there was a burn wound that had mostly healed. However, when I looked at the healing blister during the trip, it looked like a deep gashing wound with a nasty infection. It seemed like the mushrooms were warping my reality and making things way worse than they really were.

I then started to hear really loud noises. First, it sounded like a giant plane was flying right above my head. After a while, the sound seemed to come from a few yards away, and it now seemed like it was a combination of a tanker, a dumpster truck, and a jackhammer. I looked around, but I couldn't see anything to which I could attribute the noises. Up to date, I can't figure out where those noises were coming from, but I suspect there might have been some construction going on somewhere near the park, and the sound was somehow magnified when the winds shifted.

At this moment, I was sinking deeper into my depression and I was starting to worry about what my colleagues would think if they knew that I was the kind of guy who tripped on mushrooms. All these worst-case scenarios kept rushing through my mind.

But just as I thought I was spiraling into a bottomless pit of depression, I heard a voice, seemingly from my head, telling me to "have more faith." Just like that when the thought entered, I started to feel better again. In a single moment, my mood totally shifted and I felt my veins pumping with courage. I stood up straight, feeling a rush of energy like I was floating. Before I knew it, I was striking a superhero pause; my arms akimbo, my chest pumped outwards, and my head held high. I was smarter than I had ever been and I was in the best physical shape of my whole life.

I remembered skateboarding along the street as a child and I thought I could make all those moves without losing my breath. I saw myself getting promoted over all my colleagues and I pictured them looking at me with admiration. In a moment, I felt like I had the answer to every complicated science question in the universe. You could give me a piece of paper and I would write down the cure for cancer, and the secret to a successful Mars landing.

I stood there for a while, filled with joy. The water

cascading near my feet didn't scare me anymore. I stepped into the water and let it wash over my legs for a few minutes. The tide had completely turned around and I was in a great head space again.

After a while, we left the stream, and this time, we were able to find our way back to the non-restricted area (we heard some children shouting in the distance and we just followed the voices). We went back to the car; we were both still tripping, but my friend was totally confident that he could drive.

I asked to see his eyes; I saw that his pupils were dilated. I refused to let him drive, so we just sat in the car for a while and listened to music. We talked about how our jobs sucked, and about our philosophies and life in general. I thought I was really coming off smart in that conversation like every word I uttered was a nugget of wisdom handed down by the gods.

We finally drove back to my friend's house and we waited out the remainder of our trips there. Towards the end of the trip, his mother and sister stopped by to visit, and we tried really hard to act like everything was okay. I think they both suspected that something was off, but none of them said anything about it; they just gave us questioning glances.

My trip wasn't what I had expected; a huge chunk of it seemed negative, but in the end, I think it was a great experience altogether. I would try tripping on mushrooms again, but next time, I'll do it in a quiet place with less stimulation.

3

4-GRAM TRIP LEADS TO WEIRD HALLUCINATIONS AND A SERIES OF EPIPHANIES

I had quite a bit of fun on magic mushrooms a couple of times in the past, so I decided to take things a step further. This time, I took four grams of dried cubes. I'm a bit of an amature mycologist; I grew the mushrooms myself and they came in quite well. I had just dried a decent batch and I had kept some of it for myself.

In preparation for my trip, I cleaned my living room and cleared it of all things that could potentially be harmful. I put some pillows on the couch and made sure that it was all nice and cozy. I also brought down a soft blanket to keep me warm and comfortable during the trip. Finally, I found an old bucket and placed it next to the couch; this was going to be my vomit bucket in case things took a bad turn.

When all was set, I meditated for a while to calm myself down. When I was in the right state of mind, I put on some of my favorite good-vibe songs. I was ready.

I blended the dried mushrooms and then put them in a jar, and poured in some hot water and powdered ginger. I had learned about this "shroom tea" recipe online and I had been wanting to try it for a while. I let the mix sit for about fifteen minutes before I drank it. It tasted nasty, so I chugged it just to get it over with.

The trip kicked in twenty minutes later and it hit me hard, like a ton of bricks. I started seeing patterns on the walls; at first, they were mild, but then they became more vivid, and they started moving and vibrating vigorously. It was quite a beautiful sight, but I knew that was just the beginning.

I started to feel some tension building up, first in my jaw, and then on the left side of my neck. At first, I thought it was a physical problem, but then the tension spread to my eyebrow, and I realized that it must be about something different.

After thinking about the tension for a while, I concluded that it must have come about as a result of my *perception*. I had an epiphany about how perception works: "Perception," I thought, "is such a simple thing, yet it counts for so much in our lives."

Perception follows a simple and predictable pattern. First, we experience something through our senses. Then, in a split second, we make a judgment as to whether that thing is good or bad. If we think it's good, we make a mental note of it, or we express our opinions out loud, and we are done with it.

However, in cases where we make the judgment that something is bad, we may deal with it in one of three ways: The first possibility is that we deal with it properly, like a rational adult – which rarely happens. The second way to deal with it is by burying it deep in our subconscious and it becomes a trigger for the negative emotions that we experience from time to time. The third possibility is that we store whatever bad thing we've experienced in our bodies, in the form of tension.

It seemed to me that the tension in my neck, jaw, and brow, had psychological origins; the mushroom trip had only served to magnify it and to bring it to my attention. To me, this meant that from that moment on, I needed to deal with everyday stressful situations in a healthier way, rather than letting them weigh me down.

About thirty minutes into the trip, I started to "see" sound-waves. Somehow, the sounds around me were being represented visually. The louder the sound, the bigger the waves. The noises started to get much louder and the visual sound-waves vibrated a lot faster. At first, it was fascinating, but as it built up, the whole thing became a real nuisance. At some point, I just wanted it all to stop, but I couldn't control any of it. I had been through such things during past trips, where the harder you try to control something, the worse it gets. So, I decided to surrender completely. Even as the sound got unbearably loud, I just tried to relax and to take it all in.

After a while, the sounds (both in their visual and auditory form) didn't bother me so much anymore. They didn't exactly subside; they just became mundane.

My attention was grabbed by something – probably an invisible entity – that was trying to pull my teeth out. For the life of me, I can't figure out what an otherworldly being would want with my teeth, but I remember feeling really weirded out as it tugged on to my incisors.

I had prepared myself to just go with the flow during the trip, so even though the tooth pulling was bewildering, I just let it happen. In fact, I encouraged the entity to go ahead and take my teeth. After a few minutes, the tugging became milder, and the entity seemingly just gave up altogether and decided to let me keep my teeth.

My focus shifted again. This time, I got frustrated with my inability to experience a break-through moment. I had been trying hard to focus for a while, but nothing was happening. I started getting angry. I opened my eyes and I started to pull at my own hair. The intense anger didn't bring me any closer to breaking through, and after a while, I thought it was getting counterproductive, so I centered myself and tried to relax again.

Suddenly, the tension in my neck changed, and it now started to feel like there was something heavy stuck inside my throat. Whatever it was, it felt very uncomfortable, and I knew it had to come out somehow. It felt like some sort of cancerous growth. It was accompanied by a dull pain and all I wanted to do was rip it out of my throat.

I started to feel like I was going insane, either that, or I was possessed by some sort of malicious energy that rendered me incapable of feeling comfortable. I decided to accept that too instead of fighting it.

The uncomfortable feeling in my throat wouldn't subside, so I figured that I could get rid of whatever was stuck there in one of two ways; I could either forcibly vomit it out, or I could scream as loudly as possible, and hopefully, I would expunge it in the process. After thinking about it for a while, I decided against both courses of action.

Just as I elected to endure the discomfort in my throat, I realized that my legs were starting to shake. At first, they shook slowly, but then they built up momentum and started to shake really rapidly. As this happened, my breathing became heavier and more intense. I felt like I was breathing several times as fast and as deep as I usually do under normal conditions.

Two or three minutes after my leg started to shake, everything stopped, and I felt really tired. The sound-waves, the uncomfortable feeling in my throat, and the shaking; they all just stopped, like a light had been turned off. I felt a bit thirsty, so I sat up, picked up a water bottle, and took a gulp of water. For the next few minutes, all I did was hold on to that bottle and say the word "done" repeatedly.

At some point, I felt like my body was losing balance, even though I was just sitting on the sofa. Then a disturbing thought entered my mind: "I'm on top of a giant rock that's hurtling through space!" This thought threw my sense of balance a lot more and I started reaching out with my arms to grab onto something. When my hand found the arm of the sofa, I felt a deep sense of relief.

I laid back on the sofa, closed my eyes, and just chilled for about thirty minutes or so. It was a profound feeling of tranquility; it felt like I was in a world of total freedom and no worries. I was completely at peace.

I then opened my eyes and I was engulfed with the feeling of love. I gazed across the room at my curtains, and for a while, I thought they had the most beautiful patterns I had ever seen. I was surrounded by total love and beauty, and it was overwhelming.

I started to cry. Tears of joy ran down my face and this indescribably warm feeling swelled up inside me. I wished I could stay in that state forever and ever.

When my feelings of joy subsided, I returned to a state of equilibrium, and I went into a very deep thinking session. I had lots of profound thoughts; I remember some of them, but I have forgotten a lot of them. Still, I felt like I was able to work out many of my emotional and philosophical issues during this phase of my trip, which lasted a couple of hours or so.

Here are a few of the deep thoughts and epiphanies that I had (while some of them may seem obvious or erroneous to a sober mind, they actually did sound deeply profound when I thought them up while under the influence of mushrooms):

- As humans, we are no different from our ape cousins (like the chimpanzees) because we don't question the nature of the universe. What if we are just an experiment? What if we are just lab rats for some higher form of life to toy with?
- Even though we have our sophisticated culture and our state of the art technologies, we still reside in the dark ages. We need to awaken, to look beyond the obvious things in order for any real change to occur in our society.
- We are one. We are all connected: This thought occurred to me when I got up from the sofa to go to the bathroom at one point. I felt connected to the ground like there were roots coming out of my feet and burrowing into the floor.
- In order to master our lives, we have to be immensely pragmatic. We waste time playing social games that don't benefit us. With pragmatism, we can get our financial situations in order, define our own purpose in life, and be rich in a way that benefits others too.
- In order to successfully enact a paradigm shift, everyone has to come along. We need to help those on the lower levels rise up too so that we can all ascend to a better paradigm.

- We shouldn't shove the things that irritate us into our subconscious. We should just express ourselves; that way, we can get rid of negative feelings.

At some point during my stream of thought, the topic of money popped into my mind. "Does money really have value? After all, it's just pieces of paper!" Then it occurred to me, "What if everyone realized that money has no value?" I felt this was the funniest thing ever and I laughed hysterically for several minutes.

Soon, the mushrooms wore off. My trip had ended, but I was left with the conviction that I ought to deal with my emotions more openly so as to avoid carrying unnecessary baggage around.

4
A HEROES JOURNEY

I have tripped on mushrooms and other psychedelics many times in the past, and I had always been curious about pushing things to the limit. I decided to take a five gram dose of magic mushrooms. Depending on who you ask, that is either a heroic dose or a borderline heroic one. Either way, I was hoping for a level five trip, and that's exactly what I got.

In preparation for my trip, I fasted for about eight hours; I had a light meal in the afternoon and I decided to skip dinner. I was planning for a late-night trip.

At half-past eleven, I set the mushrooms on the table, together with a bowl of dry crackers, a glass of orange juice, and a bottle of water. I started eating the mushrooms with the crackers (to improve the taste and texture) and I washed it down with the juice. Even with the aid of the juice and crackers, the taste was still so terrible, that I had to pause between bites to center myself again before I could take the next one. With each bite, the temptation to stop grew stronger, but I was determined to see it through, so I soldiered on.

As I was chewing at the last bite and preparing myself psychologically to swallow it, I noticed that the effects of the mushrooms had started to kick in; this startled me a bit, so I glanced over at the clock: as it turned out, I had taken an entire thirty minutes just to eat the mushrooms! Because of the nasty taste of the shrooms and my own nervousness about the trip, I totally failed to notice the come-up. One second, I wasn't tripping, and the next second, I was.

This realization made me truly scared. Throughout the day, I had in the back of my mind this crushing fear that I might have a bad trip. I felt like my instincts were telling me not to trip, but I dismissed that as sheer nervousness. My friends advised me against taking a dose that high; they filled my head with horror stories about people trying heroic doses and ending up in the emergency room or worse. Even though I had put various safety measures in place as part of my preparations, I couldn't totally get over the feeling that something might go wrong.

So, when the effects of the mushroom crept up on me, it felt like everything I had feared was coming true. I became totally convinced that this was bound to turn bad. My nervousness and anxiety started to build up, and I was on the verge of totally losing control.

As worries of getting trapped in a terror trip started to fill my mind, I remembered that I had prepared for such a scenario. I swallowed the last bit of mushroom, and I started breathing deeply and exhaling slowly as I tried to calm myself down.

The effects of the mushrooms were intensifying at this moment and I started to feel a dark, evil presence lurking over me. It was a disconcerting feeling, so I tried to make sense of it. But as I tried to focus my eyes, my visual field was suddenly populated by some of the strangest images I have ever seen. Even though my eyes were wide open, I couldn't pick out any familiar object in my room. Instead, there were shadowy patterns that seemed to hold some sort of occultist significance.

Then, an otherworldly dimension faded in, and it engulfed my entire reality. Suddenly I was somewhere else, somewhere dark and horrifying. There was a giant pyramid towering over me, and in front of it, there were Mayan warrior guards. They had stern looks on their darkened faces and there was something evil about them. I could immediately tell that they weren't exactly pleased with my presence there. It was like they were guarding something secret, and they were very pissed off that I had wandered into their dimension uninvited.

I was expecting them to harm me in some way and just as my mind started to run through worse case scenarios, I noticed a gigantic woman behind the pyramid. She also wore Mayan traditional regalia and it occurred to me that she might be what the warriors were protecting. This was her domain; she existed behind the curtain of reality and mere mortals weren't allowed to see her.

As the giant woman came into focus, I realized that she was dancing. There was something deeply sensual about the way she was moving. Her rhythm was perfect and her whole demeanor was enchanting. And yet, she felt evil and dark. I just knew somehow that she was the kind of woman that drew you in with her charms, and then devoured you. She was an enchantress, a succubus.

She terrified me. I thought that she would draw me in with her feminine wiles and I wouldn't be able to resist her magic. I thought that if I looked at her long enough, I would get hypnotized or something. So, I decided to shift my focus from her, to direct my attention towards anything but her.

I tried the best I could to redirect my attention, but it was too late. She had already hypnotized me and I couldn't break her spell through sheer willpower. Her silhouette came into sharper focus, as she danced more sensually, more energetically. It occurred to me that I couldn't possibly be her only victim or target; it seemed that her powers of seduction were immeasurable, and she could keep everyone hypnotized at the same time with little effort.

As she kept dancing, I noticed that vibrations and waves were coming from her and spreading throughout the entire extra-dimensional reality. She was the source of energy for the plane; she controlled everything. She was the goddess of this reality and all things that existed were there to serve her. She was petrifying and she invoked thoughts that could make brave men afraid to fall asleep.

This hallucination was so surreal that I felt myself freeze with fright. And then the light bulb went off; somewhere in my mind, it just clicked: She was the embodiment of fear. The fear that I had, going into the trip, had created her and not the other way around. I was afraid to let go, afraid of whatever lay ahead in my trip, and as my mind processed this information, my subconscious dealt with it by spitting out this evil, scary, mysterious ancient goddess.

She wasn't the one controlling me; my fear was. She was just a visual symbol of that fear, some sort of cosmic interpretive dancer who brought a negative emotion to life.

Upon that realization, I decided to take control. I decided to let go of my fear and to embrace the uncertainty of my trip. Just as I made that decision, the Mayan woman diffused, like a drop of ink in water, and she slowly faded away. My fear had subsided, so it was time for her to go.

My fear was replaced by a very intense urge to embrace the unknown. It felt like the mushroom was pushing me, trying to get me to let go, but I kept clinging onto reality. It was like I was at the bank of a very turbulent river, and I was supposed to dive in, but I was hesitant, trying to stay on the bank even though I knew it wasn't really an option. Losing touch with reality is not easy; you have to let go of all the things you know so that you can experience something greater.

My hesitation was no match for the five grams of mushrooms I had ingested; my reality was swept away in a tide, and I found myself floating around in a metaphysical realm.

I suddenly became aware of the fourth dimension; the hyperspace. I had read so much about it; I knew that it was either a spiritual or mental realm that could only be experienced by people whose minds were truly opened up. Still, nothing I had read could have prepared me for what I saw there.

There were disembodied entities floating all over the place. Some seemed to go about their business, indifferent towards me. Some of them turned away from me as if in a deliberate attempt to avoid interacting with me. Some of them found my presence there curious and they came towards me.

One of the beings took a particularly keen interest in me. It was floating by when it noticed me. It stopped and started talking to me. I don't think any real words were exchanged; in fact, I believe most of the communication was telepathic. It welcomed me to the dimension and it beckoned me to come along so that it could teach me about that place.

The friendly entity gave me a crash course on how to use the power of thought to navigate through the hyperspace. The whole thing was insane in retrospect, but at the moment, I felt like I was taking an orientation tour of a magical universe.

After that, my confidence levels received a bit of a boost. I felt like I knew the rules of the game, like I could let go and marvel at this incredible visual universe without a monster popping out of the shadows and swallowing me whole. I believed I have some semblance of control over my hallucinations, and that made me feel secure.

I lay back in my bed, got as comfortable as I could, and pulled the covers over my head so that I was totally buried in my duvet. Then, I just let go of everything. I stopped trying to control my thoughts, and I let my mind wander wherever it wanted to. I did the same with my body; no tightening of the muscles or clenching of the jaw; I just released myself.

That's when I experienced ego death. All that I was, everything that defined me, just washed away. Since I wasn't trying to control my body anymore, it seemed to have gained a mind of its own, and it was now contorting in bed, uncontrollably, and with no discernible rhythm.

In my ego death, I awoke on the other side, not as myself, but as pure energy. I only existed in the form of consciousness. I felt like I was an all-powerful being, maybe even a god. There was nothing that could restrain me and I seemed to possess every superpower imaginable.

I started to chant out loud: "I am awake!" My speech seemed beyond my control. It wasn't me talking; it was the energy that was the essence of my being. I kept chanting on as loudly as I could. If anyone had been in the house with me at the moment, they'd probably think that I had totally gone mad, or that I was possessed by some kind of spirit.

After a while, my chanting got so intense that I couldn't finish the entire phrase. Instead, I just kept saying "Am! Am! Am!" repeatedly. I was writhing in bed and my body, now dispossessed of my mind, kept striking strange poses. After a while, all the twisting started to feel uncomfortable, but I didn't seem to be able to stop it.

I'd find myself placing my hand on my forehead without having any idea why I was doing that. At times, it felt like I was flashing ancient gestures like certain restless ancestral spirits were guiding my actions. I just kept chanting on an on. At some point, I chanted "Am!" in a particularly high note and held it for a while like it was a song.

As my chants became more musical, I became ecstatic. I was very happy inside and I felt truly awakened. Then, I got overwhelmed by the thought that I was an all-powerful spec of energy that transcended the physical. In my mind, that made me divine. "I'm not just a god; I am God!" I felt like I had this power over humanity, over all creatures. But then, it occurred to me that if I wielded all that power, it would be within my ability to stop all human suffering.

I started to feel sad for mankind. I felt that even though I could stop everyone's suffering, I wasn't going to, because that would negate the principle of free will. All I could do was weep. I started to cry and to express deep sadness for everyone who's experienced any suffering. I kept saying "I'm sorry" over and over, as I apologized profusely for all the pain that I, as God, inflicted upon all humans.

I, as the author of the universe, knew that everything that exists serves an important purpose, and is a part of the fabric that holds the world together; pain and suffering must exist. Without pain, there is no creation. I was compassionate, but I couldn't deliver people from their suffering. I decided to send out a telepathic message to all humans, telling them to seek me if they needed solace.

I started to talk out loud, this time delivering an important prophetic message to all of mankind: "It's the start of a golden age, and going forward, all will be well", I declared. I thought that everyone around the world could hear me and that my words would bring spiritual nourishment to starving souls.

Throughout this entire phase of my trip, it did not seem to matter whether my eyes were closed or wide open. I kept seeing the same things. In fact, sometimes, I literally couldn't tell the difference. My consciousness was in a constant state of transformation, changing its very nature, as it surged with energy.

At this moment, I was shifting from one form of energy to another. I caught glimpses of multiple other realms and dimensions that I was yet to visit. I rapidly drifted through some of them, just to gain a basic understanding of what they felt like.

Moving through multiple dimensions, I realized that existence was cyclical in nature. Everything was interlinked. Each dimension had a portal to all the other ones. I had learned earlier that I was God, but with this new realization, it occurred to me that it was more complex than that: Yes, I was God, but so was everyone else. Divinity resided in me and in all creatures, living and dead, all at the same time. Just like the dimensions were interlinked, so was everything in the universe.

After contemplating the interlinked nature of the universe, I found myself in an abstract state of being. Nothing seemed to have any particular meaning or to make any sense. Things were just swirling around, blending into each other, and morphing into new things altogether. It was weird yet beautiful.

At some point, my stream of thought was interrupted and I felt like my consciousness was getting rejoined with my body. In a flash, I was reborn as a human once more. The mushroom was wearing off.

I turned in bed and looked at the clock on my nightstand. It was about a quarter to four in the morning. I could still feel the mild effects of the mushrooms, but I just knew that the crazy heroic parts of the trip were over.

I felt a sick sensation in my stomach and I rushed to the bathroom as fast as I could. I had diarrhea and I spent the next fifteen minutes or so on the toilet. When I was done, I felt totally empty. It was a complete purge; I felt that it must be symbolic. All the old parts of me, my limiting beliefs, and my fears were gone, and now I was a blank slate, waiting to be filled with new and exciting experiences.

I finally got back into bed and I spent the remainder of my trip thinking about my friends and family. I sent them love and positive thoughts; thanks to my trip, I now believe that this gesture is not in vain. I fell asleep at some point and I woke up the next day sometime around noon, feeling totally sober.

FAQS

How long does a mushroom trip last?

When mushrooms are taken orally, in the vast majority of cases, the trip usually lasts between four to six hours. After that period, many people experience latent effects (e.g. difficulty falling asleep or just feeling a little off) for another two to six hours before things feel completely normal again.

Under normal circumstances, the trip would start anywhere between twenty and sixty minutes after ingestion of the mushroom. So, for planning purposes, it's generally safe to estimate that your trip would be over after about seven hours from the point of ingestion.

There are several factors that can influence the duration of a mushroom trip. Adding citrus to the mushrooms can hasten its uptake, so it can shorten the come up period. Ingesting mushrooms on a full stomach can slow its uptake and it can increase the come up period.

How often can I trip?

Technically, you can trip as often as you want, but it's advisable to wait about ten days between trips to avoid building up resistance to whatever dosage of mushrooms you are taking. Mushrooms have a refractory period of roughly two to eight days; that means that if you take the same concentration of mushrooms every few days, you'll get progressively lower effects, and after some time, you may get no effect at all. Waiting for ten days will allow you to return to your baseline state, which means you won't have to up the dose for subsequent trips.

When it comes to your physiological well being, it's important to note that psilocybin and psilocin (the psychoactive ingredients in mushrooms) are not neurotoxic at typical doses. That means that ingesting a few grams of mushrooms regularly won't cause any physical harm to your brain or your other organs, so you don't have to worry about that if you are a regular tripper.

What are the differences between the various methods of ingestion?

First, there are several primary methods of ingesting mushrooms: direct ingestion, the shroom tea method, the shroom smoothie method, and the citrus juice shot method. To understand their differences, let's look at them one by one:

Direct ingestion method

In this method, you would eat mushrooms just like any other food; you just have to ensure that you chew thoroughly so that it's broken down faster in the stomach.

In this method, the come-up time would be anywhere between thirty minutes and two hours, depending on whatever else is in your digestive system at the moment. If you eat mushrooms on a full stomach, it would take much longer for it to kick in.

You can use any non-alcoholic beverage you want to chase the taste of the mushrooms.

Shroom tea method

In this method, you would have to brew one cup of "tea" for every one gram of mushroom that you want to consume. Boil water and add the mushroom, then wait till it sinks all the way to the bottom of the container; that's how you would know that the infusion process is complete. Usually it takes about one hour or less. As a precaution, you should avoid boiling the mushrooms for more than an hour because that would reduce its potency. You can then cool and drink the liquid along with the remaining bits of the mushroom.

Shroom tea has a very short come-up period. However, the boiling process reduces the potency of the mushrooms, and this by extension, reduces the overall intensity of the trip.

Shroom smoothie method

This is the perfect method to use if you are primarily interested in masking the taste of the mushrooms. All you have to do is add mushrooms as an ingredient in your favourite smoothie and then blend it a couple of times on the pulse setting. Alternatively, you can just shred the mushrooms, put them in a water bottle, top it up with some juice, and then shake it thoroughly.

The come-up time is significantly reduced in this method because the body absorbs liquids faster than digesting food.

Citrus juice shroom shots (lemon tek method)

In this method, you would have to crush dried mushrooms

into powder form, put the powder in a cup, and then squeeze in two or three ounces of fresh citrus juice (preferably lemon or lime juice). You would then let the mixture sit for roughly thirty minutes before taking it in a shot.

The citric acid in lemon and lime breaks down psilocybin and turns it into psilocin; basically, the acid "digests" the shrooms right there in the glass, so it reduces the come-up time, while increasing the intensity of the trip. It also makes you peak a lot faster, and as a result, it reduces the duration of the entire trip.

What is set and setting?

Set refers to your psychological and physical preparedness at the time of the trip. *Setting* refers to your location and surroundings during the trip. To have a productive or fulfilling trip, you need to optimize your "Set and Setting".

To be in good "Set and Setting" you have to ensure that you are in a positive mood, your spirits are high, you are in a great atmosphere, you are comfortable, and if necessary, you are surrounded by positive people.

To practice good "Set and Setting", avoid ingesting mushrooms when you are nervous or anxious, when you are in an uncomfortable place, when in the company of judgmental people or people who tend to stress you out, etc. You should also make sure that you reduce your chances of harming yourself or others by putting away sharp objects.

The purpose of your trip will affect your choice of Set and Setting. For example, if you want to experience nature, then you need to be outdoors, and if you want to do some introspection and face your inner demons, you should be in a place where you won't be disturbed.

You should make sure that your purpose for the trip is

personal; if you do it to impress other people, to spite your parents, or to escape from life's challenges, there is a chance that this could backfire, and you could have a bad trip that involves being haunted by the very things you are running away from.

Should I trip alone?

If you are a total newbie where psychedelics are concerned, it's wise to have someone with you when you go on your first mushroom trip. If you are experienced, it's okay to do it, but there are things you need to consider before choosing to trip on mushrooms alone.

Tripping alone has its advantages. You have more freedom to choose how to direct your trip without having to consider other people's opinions and needs. This means that your trip is more likely to be an introspective journey of self-discovery. If that sounds good to you, then you should trip alone.

The downside of tripping alone is that you have no fail safe if things take a wrong turn. If you have a bad trip, there is no one to help you out, so you may be more likely to harm yourself. You can mitigate against that by putting dangerous objects away.

The dosage also matters here. If you are taking a powerful or heroic dose, you might want to have someone watching over you. However, if you are taking a typical dose, it's less likely that your judgement will be impaired to the point of needing help.

ALSO BY ALEX GIBBONS

Did you enjoy the book or learn something new? It really helps out small publishers like Alex if you could leave a quick review on Amazon so others in the community can also find the book!

Want to chill and experience the benefits of mindfulness? Want to do something productive while watching random videos on YouTube?

Get this fun stoner themed coloring book to scribble on for your next trip. Search for 'Alex Gibbons Stoner Coloring Book' on Amazon to get yours now!

Thinking about taking other magical drugs? Ever wondered what exactly happens when you take them? Want to make sure you don't have a bad trip?

If you want to read more about the history, origins and effects of Magic Mushrooms, LSD/Acid or DMT, search for 'The Psychedelic Bible' on Amazon!

For daily posts on all things Psychedelic, follow us on Instagram @Psychedelic.curiosity

www.ingramcontent.com/pod-product-compliance
Lightning Source LLC
Chambersburg PA
CBHW021133080526
44587CB00012B/1269